The Gum Trees of Kerikeri

The Gum Trees of Kerikeri

Lynn Jenner

OTAGO UNIVERSITY PRESS
TE WHARE TĀ O ŌTĀKOU WHAKAIHU WAKA

1.

The land I live on was a kauri forest for centuries, then in the late nineteenth century it was a kauri gumfield, then a mandarin orchard; part of a dairy farm in the 1950s, a tamarillo orchard in the 1970s, and a lavender farm in the 1980s: now it is home to four people, lots of ornamental trees, a vegetable garden, two old plum trees, travellers from New Zealand and other countries; and sometimes, when the neighbours are short of feed, four pretty horses. Around the perimeter gum trees planted in the 1930s as shelter for the mandarins send down coloured leaves and spears that would pierce your chest. Last summer a California quail with a topknot came onto the deck in the late afternoon, faced the lounge window and pecked the glass hundreds and hundreds of times. We thought perhaps he was trying to drive off another quail and did not realise that the bird in the window was him.

2.

If we meet a car while we are walking on our road, we do the neighbour wave. In return the person driving lifts one hand off the steering wheel and holds it up until we have passed, or, if they are feeling a little more grudging, they lift two fingers but not the whole hand. When a visitor from Wellington asked if the person I waved to was a friend I said not yet. Bill Parkes, a doctor who came to Hokianga in 1956, was surprised when the locals waved to him as he drove the unsealed roads on his way to Rawene Hospital; he was even more surprised at how welcoming this waving felt and could hardly believe that he didn't have to do anything except be there to be acknowledged in this way. For this and other reasons Bill Parkes dug in, started wearing shorts and sandals to work, bought a little boat, and became a part of things.

3.

In spring the poplar trees in Ness Road have soft new leaves; I stop walking and listen to them gossiping. I would like to lie down in the shade, close my eyes, and swim in their secrets like I used to beside the Waikanae River. My friend and I would find some place just off the path, lie side by side for a while listening to the river and the trees, then get up, say nothing, and keep on walking. As Tomas Tranströmer says, whoever lies on their back under huge trees is also up in them. But Ness Road is a farm road in Northland and a grey-haired woman lying down on the grass verge would not last long: dogs would find me, sniff my face, and everyone would want to help.

4.

Yesterday a farmer from Peria asked me what I thought of the gum trees of Kerikeri and I told him I had mixed feelings about them, although I knew that some people had strong views. The farmer told me that when he bought land in 1970, it had already been cleared of bush. Twenty years seemed a long time to him then, and he needed shelter for his sheep and cows, so he had planted gums, but now, as an older man, he wishes he had been patient enough to plant native trees instead. Last year a few gum trees on land near Kororipo Pā were spray-painted and slashed with axes because they are not natives and, on a different site, a private developer has felled hundreds of gums to make way for 300 houses. From the window of the Cornerstone Church, which is on the site of the former colonial courthouse, I watch the trunks being trucked out, all cut to the same length and sold by the metre, for firewood.

5.

At the yard where they sell the firewood a woman comes out of a small building to show us the wood for sale, then, once we have decided how much to buy, she takes us into the building to write down our address. It is homely in there: a green and white Shacklock coal range in one corner radiates heat and a couple of cast iron frying pans on the top have remnants of recently fried chops and eggs. Fifty years ago, when Dunedin had factories that made things, Uncle Jack worked in the Shacklock factory making doors for ovens, which has left me with a soft spot for the word Shacklock written in cursive on white enamel, and the particular comfort that a coal range provides. Later in the afternoon the man who delivered the wood told us he had given us some extra because some of the wood got a bit wet in the last cyclone, and not to bother paying till we had checked the wood and were happy with it. He also told us that before he started cutting firewood he was a chef and had once spent $1000 on a 26-course degustation at Noma in Copenhagen; after that we stood in the winter sun and discussed recipes for cooking venison.

6.

A sign on the rail trail from Ōkaihau to Opua says the railway was built in the early twentieth century to take logs from the north to Auckland, and to carry people to and from the north. There was a plan to take the railway all the way to Kaitaia, but that never happened: once the idea of the railway stopped growing, the railway itself began slowly to die, until the service to Ōkaihau stopped altogether in the 1980s. Looking at the pictures of the trains I felt as if I was looking at photographs of people to whom I am related but did not know in their prime. Charles Brasch once saw a steam engine in a dream; she was his mother: she came from nowhere, crossed the road, and went back down to nowhere; as we walked the trail through the ginger, the jasmine and the gorse, I heard a heavy engine behind me and I turned, half hoping that I would see a stylish green diesel locomotive grinding up the hill. But there was no train.

7.

Make yourselves at home, our neighbour said from his seat on the couch, his legs straight out in front on a stool; the sky dark, the room dark, the TV screen dark; nothing on the table beside him, not even a cup. We dragged over a couple of dining room chairs and sat near him expecting to hear hospital stories of stodgy food and painkillers and which nurses were kind. We heard instead that the men in the ward were so hungry they sent one of their visitors out for McDonald's, and there was a nurse our neighbour was sure had been stoned; the way that nurse looked around and never spoke, and their vague manner, were the signs. One night in Afghanistan in the late 1970s our neighbour had stayed in a house with two men who toasted hashish in their frying pan and inhaled the smoke through rolled up paper cones, and just being in the room was enough to get very stoned, and they had ruined that country: I wasn't sure if our neighbour meant the Taliban, the Russians, the opium traders or the Americans; but anyway, after Afghanistan, he and his blonde girlfriend from a farm near Gisborne went to Cairo, and men kept touching her and reaching their hands into his pockets to take his money, but he found a way of walking in front of his girlfriend, taking short steps because she was not as tall as him, and he flapped his arms like wings to keep the men away from her. How long do you need to keep your leg up, we asked; another week at least, our neighbour said, and I thought of Scheherazade who told a thousand stories to pass a thousand nights.

8.

At the Waipapa intersection on State Highway 10, opposite the Pioneer Restaurant and Bar, the BP petrol station, Bay of Islands Fish and Chips and Little Asia are two sculptures cut from sheets of iron. A woman with a child on her back bends over a pot on the fire, a child stands close to her and, a little way away, a man has an axe raised, ready to split a kauri log. Across the road is a man with a spear and a spade to dig for kauri gum. The oxidised metal colour of the figures gives them a warm quality. I wonder if I will ever meet the people who commissioned these sculptures and what I would say to them if I did, and what difference my words would make because the sculptures would still be there, radiating virtue.

9.

A farmer on *Country Calendar* pointed to the hills in the distance covered with pines and said that these trees would be an income for his son, wool now being almost worthless and the land too steep for any other kind of farming. His family had farmed this land for five generations, he said with pride, then he pointed to a single kahikatea on a ridge, in front of the pines, the sole remnant of bush that used to cover the land. I don't know how trees feel or even if they have a sense like that, but I imagined a great aloneness. The farmer held his arms out wide and said this kahikatea was five hundred years old and its trunk was six metres in circumference; there was something different in his voice then, perhaps surprise, or some form of admiration. A friend told me recently that every biblical scholar she had studied had referred to a tree somewhere in their writing, and I told her that the British soldiers fighting in the Northern War soon learned that every tree was a friend.

10.

Yesterday police officers were stopping every car on Waipapa Road near Kerikeri. When it was my turn a tall, fair-haired officer about 30 years old pushed a breath tester towards me. 'Say 12345,' he said, and as I spoke I saw a tattoo on his arm which said RAGE. In times gone by it was thought that a jewel the colour of blood could cure a disease of the blood or a picture of the sun could warm a person: this was called 'sympathy'. If the fair-haired officer's arm came in the car window of a person with rage in their gut, there might be an activation, but there would be no sympathy in the court.

11.

Before they leave for war, soldiers smile for their mothers and look proud, sitting or standing next to a potted palm, slightly awkward in their uniforms. In the field the men are all concentration, putting chunks of food into their mouths, moving guns, or standing beside their jeeps, uniforms dirty and wrinkled; not enough food and not enough sleep; death or terrible wounds right beside them yesterday, and tomorrow again, but today they are alive: the soldiers of Ukraine look like this. Standing face to face with a general, getting a medal pinned to their tunic, their eyes are hooded and their thoughts their own. Most prisoners of war drop their heads, try not to catch anyone's eye: a few, the ones with sharp glittering eyes, are waiting for the chance to kill someone. When a man with those eyes walks past me on the street, I look away and try to be invisible, but once at home and safe, I think about the war that man is fighting.

12.

Standing on the roundabout on Highway 10 on a Saturday morning, waving our 'Stop the Genocide' and our 'Free Palestine' flags, the 25 of us are a bit of a spectacle. Old people, young people, dogs and children stare at us from inside new cars and little old cars, utes with huge exhaust pipes, dirty farm trucks, ambulances and police cars. Nearly half the drivers toot their horn and wave; the occasional person gives us the finger, the thumbs down, or a gesture that says we are crazy, but lots of the drivers and passengers and all the dogs just look. They open their eyes wide and stare at us for the whole time it takes to go around the roundabout and pass by; then they are gone and who knows what they will think about for the rest of this day. We are the humans who live here, all of us parts of the sometimes kind and sometimes frightening whole.

13.

During their week-long stay at our cousins' Airbnb cottage the couple from Whangārei asked for a new roll of clingfilm, a roll of tinfoil and a packet of Ziploc bags. No guests had ever asked for these things before and we had some discussion about what these people were doing to need so many wrappings and whether it was reasonable to expect hosts to supply this kind of item. In rating their experience, the couple from Whangārei said their stay in the cottage had been just the retreat they needed and had given them a chance to make memories. We think they baked their memories in the oven, waited for them to cool, rolled them in clingfilm, then tinfoil, and took them home in Ziploc bags.

14.

Insects fly low and fast from one end to the other of the field of white and yellow flowers that a farmer would call weeds. On the deck, right by the window, a giant quail on one leg drops shit, two smaller female quails on the edge of the deck watch him, and two quarter-sized quails climb with difficulty over the legs of the outside chairs. A hawk flies her usual beat from east to west and back again, looking for anything small and soft and undefended; two rosellas from the tōtara tree come in low and disappear into the flowers: somewhere in there they have a nest. Three little rabbits from the colony under the house search around the young trees for an unprotected trunk to chew; a single pūkeko comes out of the flowers and heads towards the young trees with his high-stepping walk. And now you, running and waving your arms, yelling 'You're not welcome here!' at the pūkeko and perhaps the rabbits too.

15.

On the path through the bush one day a tour group from a cruise ship pass us. They wear white clothes with no signs of wear or dirt, and they walk in single file, each person the same distance from the one in front, a man speaking into their headsets telling them something; maybe about the trees, maybe not to fall behind or make eye contact with the locals. Behind them they leave a trail of expensive smells. Last night a line of SpaceX satellites rose in the southwest, crossed the sky in a low arc and disappeared to the east leaving no trace, each light the same distance from the one in front and moving at a steady pace, like a military convoy. Somewhere in a bunker an engineer speaks to the satellites in their own language, tells each of them their fate is to keep going and never deviate until the end, when their light will fall exhausted from the sky and another will join, so that the convoy never changes.

16.

Walking up through the Hongi Hika reserve from Kororipo Pā is peaceful and cool. Red and yellow gum leaves cover the path and I picture them as a fabric I would love to wear. There is silence at first, but then I hear a digger working and just one tūī who follows us in the trees beside the path. A poet told me that when you cut down a gum tree, new trunks grow from the stump, and this is called 'compensatory growth'. I had noticed gum trees with several trunks rising from the same base, and now I understood. Perhaps someone had tried to fell the tree, or it had been damaged by a storm, and when it couldn't grow straight up the tree grew more trunks; and in case that didn't work, it gave a hundred seeds to the east wind, and those seeds made ten new saplings all around the base.

17.

When my great-grandfather Isaac Boock travelled from Krakow to Wellington in 1879 he did not know what the new place would be like, but he knew it was time for a radical leaving. He did not know that he would have nine children here in New Zealand, all of whom would survive childhood. He did not know that joining his fate with the British Empire would require four of his sons to fight in World War I and one to die, which is a slightly worse outcome than the one-in-five death ratio for the New Zealand troops as a whole. Between the two World Wars Isaac's remaining eight children had 20 children, one of whom was my mother. Isaac's decision to leave by himself, live in another language, and never see any of his own family again saved his future children from the Nazi Reich, and that in turn enabled the birth of around 420 children who now live in New Zealand, Australia, Israel, and probably other places too. I wonder sometimes if I would know when it is time to leave, and how many of his descendants ask themselves the same question.

18.

As we walked across the hill beside Kororipo Pā this morning towards Hongi Hika's track, the only sound was our shoes scratching through dry grass: in front of us a row of ninety-year-old gum trees; above them the cerulean sky and not a single cloud. I often have a sense of people on that track. I don't hear literal footsteps and I don't see shadows; I just feel bodies in a group, movement and goods to be carried. This morning you pointed towards the edge of the bush and whispered, 'Kōtare, on that branch, watching us.' A second kōtare flew fast and low through the trees, its wings bright blue: there was a flash of feathers on the branch near us, and then they were both gone.

19.

Fallen gum leaves are often, but not always, the shape of a feather. The leaf I picked up today is sand coloured where it has dried, has dark red edges, a dark red line up the centre, and irregular smudges of green left over from when the leaf was alive. The sand colour is warm and slightly pink, like the desert at sundown in the film of *The English Patient*. The green is like thousands of trees I saw out the window of a train in New South Wales. I did not think that leaves would be falling in January.

20.

The river trickles and burbles, running over rocks and around corners; if you live in an apartment where you hear your neighbour's TV through the wall, you might lie down on your bed and play this gentle water sound in your earbuds. The light through the trees is as clear as an emerald, as a mountain pool, as a young girl's eyes. Tūī swoop through lower branches, shining black and green in the sun; perhaps if we reached out our arms like Saint Francis, tūī would land on our upturned hands. I saw Saint Francis once, in the Wellington Hospital carpark. He was in the little box at the gate: I knew he was Saint Francis because he held out his hands and birds landed on his palms, and because he knew somehow that I had been there all night and he lifted the barrier arm and let me drive out without paying.

21.

I set an alarm to wake me at 4 am and at exactly 4:35 I see a light as bright as Venus, moving faster and with more certainty than an aeroplane. Inside that tiny bright light are six bedrooms, two bathrooms, a gym and six or seven full-sized humans who do experiments on their bodies, clean the toilets, maintain the ageing metal structure, and sometimes go outside while tied to the ship with a cord. As the light rises and then passes overhead, I hear a sound like a Tibetan singing bowl. Once the light has gone, there is silence again and I am back to being a sleepless woman standing on a wooden deck in Northland. I post my observations and experiences on the International Space Station Facebook home page: *26 January 2025. Why was there a sound like a Tibetan singing bowl as the ship passed over New Zealand?* No answer from the people in the space station, but pictures of their latest spacewalk and a link to an article about damage to the eyes of people who are in space for a long time.

22.

At the start of the relaxation part of the yoga class there is a loud clunk as my favourite yoga teacher presses the button on her 1980s portable cassette player. Then, over a background of tinny classical music, she tells us to rise up into the blue Kerikeri sky and the puffy white clouds and imagine ourselves floating above the Bay of Islands. The plonking piano and the mechanical whirring of the cassette hold me captive for a while but in the end I always go somewhere. I know I do, because at the end I come back. I don't know where we all go, but that doesn't matter because the teacher knows how to send us away and how to bring us back.

23.

Between 1465 and 1474, in the Ducal Palace in Mantua, Andrea Mantegna painted frescoes of many many angels in a bright blue sky with puffy white clouds that seem more than real. Pictures of Mantua today show the same intensely blue sky. Last week, when the yoga teacher asked us all to go outside and stand on the grass, I walked over the lawn and took a place under a tree, feeling the individual leaves of dry and stalky grass holding me just above the earth. Then I lay down on the grass, looked up and saw our Kerikeri sky, watery blue, as if soft rain had just fallen. But this summer all the water is staying in the sky and we are tapping our water tanks to see how much is left.

24.

Sometimes when walking in Pukeiti Forest you come around a corner of the track and find yourself face to face with a tree whose trunk is so big that it would take four or five people holding hands to reach around it; maybe there is a little sign at the foot telling you it is a Mātai, or a Kauri or Kahikatea; sometimes there is just a grand tree, unnamed. Sometimes the grand tree is a little distance from the path, but sometimes it is right there, beside you, so tall that it touches the sky. I always stay on the path to stop the trees from catching kauri dieback disease from spores on my shoes, but today, as I passed a great tree with a rough scaly trunk right on the path, I reached out and touched it with my hand, palm open to feel I-do-not-know-what. Its bark was hard, nothing like animal skin: I did not feel its life as you feel the heartbeat of an animal, but as something large and enduring, part of a world of ferns and vines and birds and other great beings. Zhou Zuoren said that we should observe the people who live in this world and how they think, and we should not be surprised if it turns out that all people want to talk about is floating logs and the ghosts of people who drowned in rivers.

25.

People talk about the degradation of the earth, but mostly they do not spell out what they see coming so as not to scare the rest of us. Also, there might be a big war coming and capitalism is in chaos which I always thought would be a good thing but it's costing people their jobs and makes our savings shrink. What use are romance novels, murder mysteries, poetry about trees, short stories about toxic relationships and eco projects in wealthy neighbourhoods in a situation like this? I like to walk up hills and watch what the birds are doing. That doesn't change anything either, but it's real, including the tree trunks marked with pink paint and the rat traps.

26.

In Anne Tyler's 2018 novel *Clock Dance*, Willa complains to her friend Denise that she is unlikely to have grandchildren because of the way her children live. Denise consoles her by saying that if you don't have grandchildren you won't have to worry about them going through the death of the planet, but a few pages on Willa decides that she deserves grandchildren, even though these children 'would have to deal with the death of the planet'. Willa talks as if her grandchildren will take the death of the planet in their stride, like when your car breaks down on the side of the road, but you call for help and someone comes: it costs a lot but you don't mind because they fix the problem and then you are back on the road. That evening, still preoccupied by the fate of Willa's grandchildren, I ask if you would have a baby now and you say, 'Yes, every human being is going to die of something, and anyway, people have always launched their babies into the future, hoping for the best': you call this optimism, but I am not persuaded. Days later I am still stuck, lost between the author and her character, optimism and insouciance; not knowing whether to look to science for help, hope that the strength of peoples' love for their children will somehow save the planet, or just watch Series 5 of *Yellowstone* and then all the different versions of *Pride and Prejudice*, one after the other.

27.

Henning Mankell's detective, Kurt Wallander, holds team meetings, directs his staff, squabbles with his bosses and works till he drops from exhaustion. Apart from occasional moments of doubt, he is confident that if he applies his tried-and-true investigation method he will eventually find out who carried out the crime, thereby satisfying the professional requirements of the role. Privately though he wonders if he has become a kitschy detective. This word has travelled a long way from its origin, so it is not clear to me whether he sees himself as overly eccentric, or as mawkishly emotional. Regardless of Mankell's intended meaning, and the nuances provided by translation, I would like to pour Inspector Wallander a cup of coffee, cut him a piece of cake and tell him that kitsch now has a certain high-brow appeal and offers its own form of comfort.

28.

At first there is only a dead body and two or three scraps of information which do not add up to any kind of explanation of what has happened. In the middle of the enquiry Inspector Wallander might have 10 or 15 pieces of information, but he still doesn't know what connects them, which leads him to despair, because this is Swedish noir and on top of that it is always winter and Wallander is lonely and has diabetes and never sleeps and eats greasy burgers and drinks too much and just imagine the state of his microbiome. At this stage, when things are going nowhere, he orders his team members into a room, shuts the door, offers them coffee and stale pastries, recites the pieces of information, tells them that no theory is either true or not true, and makes everyone sit for a while in stillness until there is white space in their heads. They have not experienced the answer yet, he says, but white space is a way station they must pass through on the road.

29.

Our vacuum cleaner used to belong to a man whose name was something like Reg. Ten years ago we happened to be walking past this man's room on the day that he was leaving to go into a Rest Home and, eyes full of unshed tears and mouth pulled tight, he offered us his vacuum cleaner. We said yes and quickly put it in the car because it was a European make and much better than we could afford. The vacuum cleaner still sucks well but it is heavy to carry around, you have to plug in the cord in each room, and its little round body is held together with duct tape. Recently, when I suggested that we get one of those new stick vacuum cleaners, you said no, you were quite happy to keep using the one we have; and since you keep me too, despite certain inconveniences, I have nothing more to say about the vacuum cleaner.

30.

On the night of the summer solstice, you called me to come and see the stars: so many, and some so bright. 'Take my arm,' you said, knowing that sometimes my feet do not touch the ground and loving me no less for that. 'There is Orion's belt,' you said, 'and there's the Southern Cross,' and I said I saw a star disappear and reappear in another place, and what if we are witnessing the end of the world. And you just held my arm and said nothing because what could we do at the end of the world except stand together. Then we saw a falling star and because it was on our right and not our left, which would be a bad omen, we were reassured.

31.

I sleep with my curtains open. Around 1:30 I wake to a dull blue sky with lumpy clouds crossing from the east; on the fence line gum trees are in full silhouette, their branches waving in the wind; casuarinas are tall dark trunks, and all the birds are in their beds. There is the moon, high in the sky, making these shadows with its white light. Standing on the grass in my tee shirt, I am part of a long chain of women drawn to the moon. I bathe in the cool silver light, my skin pleasure and my night wonder.

32.

Silver-plate moon. High-in-the-sky moon. Light-as-bright-as-day-but-cold moon. Feral-cat-with-a-bird-in-its-mouth wild moon. Time-to-sow-the-carrots-for-winter practical moon.

33.

Someone asked me recently if I had written any poems about redemption and deliverance. I said, no, I do not see a Promised Land, in literal or metaphorical form. That sounded a bit pompous so I asked a wise friend, do you see redemption and deliverance anywhere, and he said if they are anywhere it would be in relationship with others. In 1925, Zhou Zuoren said if there was even one moment when we stopped treating others and ourselves as sheep or utensils, we might survive; he does not know how to change this habit of cruelty, he says, but he writes his thoughts and publishes them. And now, in this time, I read them.

34.

In the poem 'Zhaozhou Asks About the Great Death', Richard von Sturmer and his father-in-law are driving together back to the Rest Home when the old man asks what would happen if they just kept going. Such a delicate opening of the topic. My father-in-law put the matter much more directly. 'Take me home,' he said, after the gathering at the Stratford R.S.A. to toast his eightieth birthday, and in response we said, 'You need to be in the Rest Home because we can't look after you,' but we were ashamed of ourselves. In the poem, after the question is posed von Sturmer imagines a long car trip ending at Te Rerenga Wairua, but I am dying to know whether in real life he spoke or let his father-in-law's words hover in the space between them because there is no kind and honest answer to that question.

35.

I woke up this morning thinking about a friend who, in 2004, asked me to be a godparent for her baby girl. I assumed, although I never asked, that my friend was at least 90% joking. I didn't believe in god, I assumed she didn't either, and I thought godparents had only a spiritual and ceremonial role: I wouldn't be sponsoring the child into a religious life so . . . (and there is the break), when I moved to another city I visited once or twice, then started working on my own new life, which was terrifying and at the same time miraculous. In the time it took for her baby to become a woman, my new life came and went. My friend's future with her baby girl, which went better and worse than she could ever have imagined, turned out to have nothing to do with god or religion and everything to do with cooking, washing clothes, listening to music, waiting out tantrums, growing vegetables and making connections with people who understood the importance of those things.

36.

Last summer, in the garden of a house I was visiting, I saw a rough clay sculpture of a man sitting on a beast: the label beside it said, 'Riding the Ox Home'. I stood and looked at the sculpture for a long time, not knowing anything of its meaning, but in the bright sun, in that little corner of the garden, the statue took on significance. In the height of summer, when we turn off Highway 10 into the road that leads us home, the road becomes a tunnel. The sides are tall rattling bamboo and jacaranda trees, a line of yellow daisies shows the way, and the car, with me in it, moves at 80 kilometres an hour towards the point of disappearance. Fallen purple flowers, yellow daisies in the sunlight; yes, the ride home is this beautiful.

37.

I heard of a man who, returning from England after the war, broke down and cried when he saw the Southern Cross because that meant he had survived; he had no job and no money but he would soon be home and could make a life. I receive notifications to tell me when the International Space Station will next be visible from my location, and I am open to the idea that a satellite could be as meaningful in 2025 as a constellation in 1945. One night I saw white lights both natural and engineered and was rewarded with a gentle but significant surge in happiness. 'Consolation has to be discovered'; that's what the patriarch of the Yellowstone Ranch said when his daughter told him he looked sad, sitting in his armchair, drinking whiskey. You can ask for notifications; sometimes you see lights, but you cannot mount a grid search for happiness as you would for a tramper lost in the bush.

38.

A poet once told me that what frightened him most about death was nothingness. I had always thought him fearless because, in his poems, he excavates aloneness over and over again, as if by doing this he could get used to it; and more than that, as if familiarity would be some consolation. In his book *Affinities*, Brian Dillon says that affinities can remain unthought until two things are placed together and you are forced to see where they connect or do not. The poet who writes about desolation sits his grandchildren on his knee whenever he can catch them and reads them stories where a wolf hides in the trees or a mother dies. No-one has ever asked him why he does this.

39.

The white rectangles on a black background and the empty rectangles with white borders in Colin McCahon's *Angels and Bed* are said to be loosely based on the hallway of his villa, as seen in a spiritual state. Shortly before painting this series McCahon was found one day lying in a foetal position on the hallway floor. Perhaps, as he lay there, he had travelled past the white borders into absence and silence and slight negative pressure. That sounds frightening, but in fact my experience of the empty rectangles with the white borders is of refreshment, like the lingering effect of cool water on a hot night. After that, who knows where the road goes.

40.

When it is time in the service for personal prayer, I bring to mind people I know are suffering, then people I do not know, who are suffering; I wish for all their suffering to end, and when that is done, I breathe slowly in and out until we move on. Once, when someone I loved was somewhere between life and death, I asked the community to pray for him. I don't know if it helped him, but something warm and strengthening came and wrapped itself around me like wool next to the skin as I waited to see what would happen. When the yoga teacher tells us to send our ōms from the meeting room to the world to make peace, I listen to the vibration of our voices, and I think of the yogis who say the power of meditation is so great that they can levitate. There are photographs of them, cross-legged, hovering in the air, often in a beautiful place and with a stick in one hand. I am sure these pictures are mostly fake but one or two may be real because they were taken in the 1970s, when such a thing could have been possible, although only in India or California.

41.

Our talk has no official beginning, no structure and no official end: it starts when the first person says what has been on her mind; that could be the problem of finding a parking place at the supermarket at New Year, or it could be that she has planned a trip and her husband doesn't want to go; no-one is criticised or blamed, including the husband: our conversation is a river with eddies and currents. We have children who fight with us as though we were the enemy; men who have taken themselves off to other countries and left us with mortgages; we have diseases with scary names: this is deep water but we are not scared of deep water. We make gardens, we paint, we write songs and poems, we record stories from the past and we create adventures for ourselves so that our spirit won't slowly die: there are cool shady pools in this river. We are not optimistic for the earth and its people, but we think the best idea is to be as optimistic as possible in our personal lives. Someone always says that and although we all look a bit shifty and our eyes slide away, we nod.

42.

In the back seat of the car my friend and I talk about Rebecca Solnit's book, *Recollections of My Non-Existence*; specifically her description of the ways women are attacked with violence and by denial of space and significance, all of this having a long history. We agree that none of what Solnit says is untrue, and that we have, ourselves, seen proof. Experience is a double-edged sword though, my friend says; she decided not to tell a doctor exactly what had happened and how it had affected her because these experiences can so easily be turned into evidence of craziness. Solnit talks about how her knowledge of the dangers of women's lives affected her; how it stopped her sleeping, made her wish her whole body was covered with armour, made her insides burn up with anger. Cosy in the back seat, under the hum of the engine, my friend and I talk about how we try to live good lives, with this dark knowledge but not overpowered by it.

43.

When Officer Juarez, a rookie in the LAPD, tells Officer Nolan, her training officer, that she has a bad feeling about a vehicle, he tells her to be quiet. The higher pitched sounds of a woman's voice and the uncontrolled nature of her statements are, as Anne Carson says in *The Gender of Sound*, just plain bad to hear. But Officer Nolan is the nicest guy in *The Rookie* so to make up for his harsh slap-down he tries to reinterpret the emotions and images that come out of Officer Juarez's mouth to make them fit into his system of observation and logic. Officer Juarez shows no interest in these translations or his instruction to be quiet and keeps on sharing her dreams and her astrological knowledge, both of which turn out to be useful in saving lives and catching bad guys. In this 2022 TV version of life, a woman wins the right to talk by keeping on talking.

44.

Sam has big breasts (she calls them tits) and a big stomach. Of all the ways I could describe her I mention that first because when I watched her in *Somebody Somewhere* I felt as though her large body was the main character: ponderous, a bit shameful and vulnerable. I could have said that Sam is the daughter of a Kansas corn farmer, that her mother is an alcoholic, her sister has just died of breast cancer, she has a dead-end job, she is desperate for someone to touch her, and that she has a motherfucker of a singing voice, but I didn't: I used her shape to describe her. When Sam and her friend Joel started walking 10,000 steps each day I thought, 'Maybe we are going to see Sam getting thinner?' and then I thought, 'I want her to get thin because that would be some sort of happy ending.' But Sam doesn't get thinner; she keeps eating ultra-processed snacks and drinking a lot, and even though part of me wants her to meet someone and find love, that doesn't happen either: at the end of Series 2 she is still the same shape and as 'highly strung' and 'emotional' as ever, which a different part of me is pleased about.

45.

One poet says: huge animals such as whales, silence, solitary walks, standing beside a fire watching sparks fly up to heaven, matter, enchantment, awe, human experience, invitations to act, humanity, compassion, poetry of the inward self, a child, the little things that pop unbidden into a poem, and joining with others all give us a sense of the sacred. Another poet says her ideas on this question change all the time. A third poet says the hospitality of the earth, the foundation of everything, is all the sacred he needs. A fourth says they were not able to speak about this, or anything else, until they had found a community. A famous French philosopher says making art is a spiritual practice, a view which I outlined once to a rabbi, receiving a definite side-eye for my trouble.

46.

At the launch of *Te Moana o Reo*, an anthology of the languages of Aotearoa, writers read poems and short prose pieces about their languages and cultures. From these readings I learned that to talk about mother tongues and cultures, you must talk about memory, and to talk about memory, you must talk about mothers, fathers and grannies: the smell of their soap and hair dye, the taste of oranges, the steam from warm white porridge, the name of a cow, and being called for a glass of milk by a name that only your grannie used. If a grey bird with a white face appears when you think of your father, you must name that bird. I learned that attention itself is a form of tenderness. I learned that these words tell us about feelings for which there are no names, and I remembered again that as long as you speak of these things, they will not be forgotten.

47.

Li-Young Lee says that whenever he is writing a poem, he feels as if the whole future of the universe depends on that poem and as he tells us this, he laughs a bit at how grandiose that sounds. But he is not cowed: poetry deals with the whole human being, he says, even the parts of ourselves that we don't like, and feeling all of ourselves makes us better people. To be of interest to him, the words of a poem must be fresh and the images pregnant. That is his word: 'pregnant'. You can be part of nature, you can be looking at nature, you can be talking about the best or the worst times, he says, as long as there is an uncovering.

48.

Carolyn Forché says many American poets write about personality, not the self. If I write a Tibetan bowl that sings and dies away; if I write a psalm, a repetition with didactic intent, a rectangle with black edges and nothing inside; if I write one leaf, is that personality or self? All that autobiographical material that pours out – the dress I wore on my first day of school, the friendship that dies because of my neglect, my great-grandfather from Poland – there is attention in it; there is storytelling, there is even compassion, but there is no uncovering, no new understanding rising up from this writing. Kerikeri is a place where the Stone Store the missionaries built to contain their shoes and guns is a source of unselfconscious pride; Kerikeri is The Colonial House Motel. Between the Stone Store and the grassy hill of Kororipo Pā I hear footsteps on the old wooden bridge, but when I look there is only a perfect inlet, parked cars and a Heritage New Zealand plaque.

49.

Colin McCahon's painting *The Flight from Egypt* has six panels, each made up of two orange shapes on a black background with the words 'the flight from Egypt', 'when do we start', 'I am tired', and 'when do we get there' in cursive script. These words could be Moses' discontented followers, children on a long car journey, or someone considering their life at particular moments. 'The desert' could be any harsh place, or a simple statement of where the tribes found themselves. 'A big tree offers shade' could be any moment of respite. 'Is this the Promised Land?' could be Moses looking down on Canaan from the top of the mountain, a child crying in a bombed-out city or it could be the artist wondering if all his labour has been worthwhile: whatever this question means, it is full of pain.

50.

After the latest cyclone which came in autumn instead of summer, the river has spread out in some places, taken a bit of its bank, and settled into a new life as a slow, dignified and larger river. In other places there is still just too much water and the river runs fast, falls over itself. Six ducks in a row on a log, their orange feet holding on tight as they float downstream faster than any duck has travelled before. From a hundred metres away we hear the waterfall, beating like a drum. Visitors take selfies with the waterfall in the background, but with the river in these moods, we keep well away.

51.

After 10 days of rain the sun is out; light and warmth feel like a great power for good. I see six doves pecking in the grass. I think of Noah and the dove with the twig in its beak. And now, with the sun on my face, I think these six doves on the lawn in Kerikeri might be an omen of peace somewhere peace is needed. Sun and doves against monsters and tanks.

52.

The water of the Waihoihoi River is brown and runs with the tide towards the sea. Two orange road cones settled in the mud make me think the river is dead, but then six inanga swim by in diamond formation, their little bodies pale and conspicuous. A pied shag floats on the surface, dives and reappears fifty metres downstream – offering no clue about what might have happened underwater. Six cast iron pou, also in diamond formation, stand beside the river, together with a volcanic boulder as tall as my waist and warm to the touch. River sea fish bird [people] rock earth fire: a record of sorts.

53.

Inside the Kauri Museum at Matakohe there is an entire reconstructed boarding house where, in one of those still life rooms so common in early settler museums, two white men meet over a topographical map, which is probably not intended as a memorial to land grabbing, but the best thing about these vignettes is that you can make up your own mind what they mean. In other rooms a banker, a timber buyer and an itinerant dentist are engaged in their trades. A woman brings tea to the banker, a different woman serves the two men with the map and a third woman is dressed as a bride; in the next window she has four children. Outside a room with two women in riding habits, one three-quarter bed and an ornate commode, the sign tells us that these two Travelling Ladies have already ridden side saddle for a whole day to get to the boarding house and will catch a steamer to Auckland in the morning. I form the theory that these ladies have left behind their mothers, the unlined cabins where they grew up and the schoolhouses where they taught; that they are striking out for Sydney, then New York or London, where they will live on toast and tea, make art, visit the great galleries, go to meetings, take to the streets, hand out leaflets about women's rights, and never again have to answer personal questions.

54.

If I had my life to live again I like to think I would learn from what has happened this time: I would not work for any government, because that never really helped, although I thought it did, and I would worry less, buy less, make more and learn to love gardening. But there is the problem of conditioning. In the very last sentence of the epilogue to *Goodbye to All That*, Robert Graves says that if he had his years to live again he would probably behave in very much the same way because his conditioning in the Protestant morality of the English governing classes would not easily be overcome, despite his rebellious nature and his obsession with poetry. Inside me is a 1950s New Zealand cocktail of Pākehā-science-will-save-the-world-make-sure-you-get-an-education-because-education-keeps-you-in-the-white-collar-class-and-don't-do-bad-stuff-to-people-but look-after-yourself-first. The second time around though, even if I started with these same ingredients, the climates, social and meteorological, would be very different, so the result would definitely not be the same.

55.

Near the end of her life, searching for a way to resist the unfolding political and environmental catastrophes of these days, Ursula Le Guin suggested following Lao Tzu's 'way of water' in order to counter aggression without being subsumed in war. Water does not fight, it does not attack: water has infinite ways and is utterly opportunistic. Near the Kerikeri Inlet a track leading to the Te Wairere waterfall follows the Wairoa Stream past gentle little rapids, clear pools, and seats positioned for the momentary enjoyment of water flowing around curved riverbanks. This morning we took the Fair Weather Loop track with the river on our left, past more babbling rapids and a deep still pool where we bent over the edge and looked for eels, past a muddy pond where drips of rain from overhanging trees popped and spread in circles like rising fish, and finally over a stream small enough that we could cross it in one stride. After that crossing, we expected the river would be on our right, but somehow it was still on our left; and then there was a river on our right, and we did not think we had crossed the river again.

56.

On Monday a friend gave us a big bag of tamarillos. We had only just finished the last of the feijoas our neighbour gave us, and now, on top of everything, it's mandarin season. At yoga this week people put out trays of avocados, sweet creamy little bananas and persimmons in autumn colours, for anyone to take. People take two or three bananas for their breakfasts, maybe an avocado for their lunch and a couple of persimmons, but no-one is mad keen on persimmons. It sometimes crosses my mind that I have done nothing to deserve these gifts, but mostly I just think how sweet the fruit tastes.

Bibliography

Carson, Anne, *The Gender of Sound* (London: Spiral House, 2025)

Dillon, Brian, *Affinities: On art and fascination* (New York: New York Review Books, 2023)

Elvy, Michelle and Vaughan Rapatahana, eds, *Te Moana o Reo* (Wellington: Cuba Press, 2025)

Graves, Robert, *Goodbye to All That* (London: Penguin Modern Classics, 2001)

Kaminsky, Ilya and Kathryn Towler, eds, *A God in the House* (North Adams, MA: Tupelo Press, 2012)

McCahon, Colin, *Angels and Bed series* (1976–1977), synthetic polymer paint on paper, c. 1100 x 730mm, Auckland Art Gallery Toi o Tāmaki and private collections

McCahon, Colin, *The Flight from Egypt series* (1980), synthetic polymer paint on paper, 6 sheets, 1104 x 731mm, private collection

Parkes, Bill, *The Fair Beginning of a Time* (Whangarei: Inder Publishing, 2003)

Solnit, Rebecca, *Recollections of My Non Existence* (London: Granta Paperbacks, 2024)

Tranströmer, Tomas, 'Breathing Space July' in *The Half-Finished Heaven: The best poems of Tomas Tranströmer*, ed. and trans. Robert Bly (Minneapolis, MN: Graywolf, 2001), p. 35

Tyler, Anne, *Clock Dance* (New York: Alfred A. Knopf, 2018)

Von Sturmer, Richard, *Slender Volumes* (Auckland: Spoor Books, 2024)

Zhou, Zuoren, *Selected Essays*, trans. David E. Pollard (Hong Kong: The Chinese University Press, 2006)

Acknowledgements

Thanks to Shelley Arlidge, Sarah Barnett, Vera Dong, Alison Glenny, Jac Jenkins, Volha Kastsiuk, Bill Nelson, Tina Makereti, Rachel O'Neill, Lawrence Patchett, John Summers and Elaine Webster for feedback on early versions of these poems and for your encouragement. Thanks to Shelley Arlidge, Lynn Davidson, Alison Glenny, Michelle Elvy and Annabel Wilson for feedback on the manuscript at various stages. Thanks to everyone at Otago University Press for their support and for producing such a fine book, thanks to my daughter-in-law Charlotte McCrae for the cover design and thanks to Aaron McLean for the author photo. Thanks to Alan Brown and Trish Miles for coffee, quizzes and for encouragement to come to Northland and thanks to Tony Pine for everything.

Published by Otago University Press
Te Whare Tā o Ōtākou Whakaihu Waka
533 Castle Street
Dunedin, New Zealand
university.press@otago.ac.nz
www.oup.nz

First published 2026

ISBN 978-1-99-134818-0

A catalogue record for this book is available from the National Library of New Zealand.

Editor: Megan Kitching
Cover: Charlotte McCrae

Printed in New Zealand by Yourbooks